Also by Lucie Brock-Broido

THE MASTER LETTERS 1995
A HUNGER 1988

Trouble in Mind

Trouble in Mind

POEMS

Lucie Brock-Broido

ALFRED A. KNOPF   NEW YORK

2014

THIS IS A BORZOI BOOK
PUBLISHED BY ALFRED A. KNOPF

www.randomhouse.com/knopf/poetry

Knopf, Borzoi Books, and the colophon are registered
trademarks of Random House, Inc.

Library of Congress Cataloging-in-Publication Data
Brock-Broido, Lucie.
Trouble in mind : poems / by Lucie Brock-Broido.— 1st ed.
p. cm.
ISBN 0-375-71022-1 (pbk)
I. Title.
PS3552.R6145T76 2004
811'.54—dc22   2003059571

Published January 22, 2004
First paperback edition October 4, 2005

FOR LUCY GREALY

(1963–2002)

Contents

(I)

The Halo That Would Not Light   3
After Raphael   4
Leaflet on Wooing   5
Still Life with Aspirin   6
Herculaneum   8
The One Theme of Which Everything Else Is a Variation   9
Periodic Table of Ethereal Elements   10
Some Details of Hell   12
Basic Poem in a Basic Tongue   13
Death as a German Expert   14

(II)

Gamine   17
Morgue Near Heaven   18
The Insignificants   19
A Lion in Winter   20
Caravansary   21
Common Swan on Ornamental Pond   22
Boy at the Border of His Own Allegory   23
Still Life with Feral Horse   24
Self-Portrait on the Grassy Knoll   25
Soul Keeping Company   26

(III)

Self-Portrait with Her Hair on Fire   29
Brochure on Eden   30
Fata Morgana   31
The Deerhunting   32
Elsewhere   34
Darwinism as Spite   35
Another Night in Khartoum   36
Lady with an Ermine   37
A Truce to Tragedy   38
Fragment on Dissembling   39

(IV)

The Halo That Lit Twice   43
Self-Portrait as Kaspar Hauser   44
Apologue on Jealousy   46
Self-Portrait in the Miraculous World, with Nimbed Ox   47
Almost a Conjuror   48
Self-Portrait with Self-Pity   49
Girl at the Border of Her Own Allegory   50
Of the Finished World   51
In Elsinore   52
Spain   53

(V)

Portrait of Lucy with Fine Nile Jar   57
The Identity of the Bridegroom   59
Self-Portrait as a Herd of One   60
Physicism   61
Pyrrhic Victory   62
Self-Portrait with Her Hair Cut Off   63
The One Thousand Days   64
Dire Wolf   66
Pamphlet on Ravening   67
Self-Deliverance by Lion   68

Notes   71
Acknowledgments   75

(ONE)

The Halo That Would Not Light

When, after many years, the raptor beak
Let loose of you,

                He dropped your tiny body
In the scarab-colored hollow

                Of a carriage, left you like a finch
Wrapped in its nest of linens wound

With linden leaves in a child's cardboard box.

Tonight the wind is hover-

Hunting as the leather seats of swings go back
And forth with no one in them

As certain and invisible as
                Red scarves silking endlessly

From a magician's hollow hat
                And the spectacular catastrophe

Of your endless childhood
                Is done.

After Raphael

Perhaps it isn't possible to say these things
Out loud without the noir

Of ardor and its plain-spoken elegance.

First, my father died. Then my mother
Did. My father died again.

After the strange storm they were ruined down
From the boughs.

                There were apples everywhere.

I am sick of not loving and not
Sleeping well, of wanting spleen.

All the Suffolk sheep stand still, eating
More, becoming fat and

                Legible. Inside, the ice assembles
Even on the crystal of the long-faced clock.

No one can read incisions sanserif; I can.
                The ghostpipes bloom at night

When no one can imagine them that way;
                I can. I am awake

Now, I can see them heathering the moors.
                The impossible post-

Raphaelite world in which I live—*is true:*
                I was little; I am middle. Will I not

                Grow old, not final
As the broken pleated falcon's wing, not

Opening, and folding in
                The smaller rain?

Leaflet on Wooing

Wanting is reposed and plump
As the hands of a Romanov child

Folded in the doeskin sashes of her lap,
Paused before the little war begins.

This one will be guttural, this war.
How is it possible to still be startled

As I am by the oblong silhouette of the coiling
Index finger of a pending death.

No longer will
Wooing be the wondrous

Thing; instead, a homely domesticity, constant
As a field of early rye and yarrow-light.

What one is fit to stand is not what one is
Given, necessarily, and not this night.

Still Life with Aspirin

There she was, the mother of me, like a lit plinth,
Heavenly, though I was reared to find this kind

Of visitation impractical; she was an unbearable detail
Of the supreme celestial map,

Of which I had been taught that there was
No such thing. Stevens wrote that

For a poem to be true, it must "come from an Ever."
If you don't fathom that, then you should not be reading this.

I was there, at Ever, and it was mostly poignant and it was cruel.
It was a subjunctive place where touch was so particular it hurt

Like a veterinarian's deep kiss, like a Jerusalem somewhere
Between fancy & imagination. I was the procuress

And the gallowglass guarding the history and turf of everything
Intimate. What word would you use to describe me now.

Imperishable? Imperishable. The stars
Appear every night in the sky. All is not well.

All Deepens. V. told me that. All deepens, which is
To say—nothing—like a mild analgesic, which is to say everything

Like Lear's three girls. Which is to say:
All of my objects have lost their correlative states

And you want to know why. Because things are just
Things now, just as everyone said they would be.

When I was there, at Ever, by the way,
I was an ascetic and unfanciful. The land there

Was all as peaceful as an aspirin, as the West Bank
Is an eternal circle of chalk and bruise and war.

You did not dream I held political
Ideals, did you. You should not be reading this and are.

Remember me in the blowsy humid corridors
Beneath the Wailing Wall, most sacred place of all.

Remember me: wishing, specific, marooned, as
One who knew exactly what the Ever was & is, a velvet school

Of courtesan, a gallows bird, all deep, all deepening.

Herculaneum

No one is bored, just barbaric
Anymore. Ash admixed with rain, which cooled

The air. How much longer will this beauty
                              Of yours last?

As if even the idea of the city
Has been lost for twenty centuries.

Don't quail like this; go
Gracefully instead.
                              Eros enters

The room like a lesser god stopped still
In the middle of a bath of oil & umbrage in

The exquisite hour.

                    No one is
Exquisite anymore. The river is so small now

It will be hard to drown
In it. And still this world's a pretty one.

                    What world.

The One Theme of Which Everything Else Is a Variation

Innocence is a catarrh of the mind, distressed,
As finite as the grade school teacher in Sierra Leone

Whose arms were axed off only at the hand, first left
And then the right, and then his mouth as he was making noise

And should be shut. A man can learn to speak again,
But never pray.
                    Wisdom is experience bundled, with prosthetic wrists.

I cannot master anymore the surgical or magical,
I do not know how the specific punishments or amputations are so

Meted out. When you delete a wing or limb
From a creature's form, it will inevitably cry out against this

Taking, but in the end it will become grievously docile,
Shut; far gone old god, you have been plain.

Let me list here the things I wish to bring with me,
For the life after this or that. I will not go back the way I came,

Carrying my clay Picasso and my tin of ginger,
Flying toward home on my way away from home.

If I am lucky in this life, here, I will go on
Being whole, and speak again old god, I will be plain.

Periodic Table of Ethereal Elements

I was not ready for your form to be cold
Ever. Even in life

You did not inhabit, necessarily, a form,
But a mind of

Rarer liquid element. It had not occurred to me
You would take

Leave and it will be winter from now on, not only
Here, in the ordinary,

But there too, in the extraordinary elegance
Of calcium and finery

And loss. Keep me

Tethered here, breathtakingly awkward and alive.

If you had a psyche it was not known to me.

If you had a figure it would be heavy ivory.

If you were a man, you would be

An autumn of black carriages filled red with leaves
From sycamore trees,

Not scattering. I was not ready for such
Earthward and unease.

Goodbye to the imperium, the rinsing wind. You, cold
As God and the great

Glassed castle in which I've lived, simply
Now a house.

A girl ago, a girlhood gone like a phial of ether
Thrown on fire—just

A little jump of flame, like grief, or,

Like a penicillin that has lost its skill at killing
Off, it then is gone.

Some Details of Hell

It is time now to turn off the devices in the wing
And listen to the rain. It is time, now, to sit still

And run your finger along the suprasternum of
The truth as it arches above the viscera, and finally.

It is a time when wires & catheters marked "single use"
Have most certainly been used before: cleansed

And sterilized, but having spent time in someone
Else's heart, they have been contaminant and

Ruined. I was strong and could lift half
Of everything. I was powerful and could be alive

And lithe as tiny scissors used
To cut out tissue in a human which had gone wrong.

Hell is a world of its own, with its own
Towns and country-side. There I stayed beside your nearly

Warm-blooded form like a brook mink in the clutch
Of a slightly larger animal and sat still, having

Spent a moment in someone else's marrow,
A diaphanoscope, catastrophic as the good love

Of a tea-stained bride abroad in the rain
Of saxifrage and clove, tomorrowing.

Basic Poem in a Basic Tongue

Here is the maudlin petty bourgeoisie of ruin.

A sullen pity-craft before the fallows of Allhallowmas.

The aristocracy in one green cortège at the registry of Vehicle and Animus.

A muster of pale stars stationed like gazelles just looking-up,

                                        Before the rustle of the coming kill.

At home, the hoi polloi keep tendering the books of Job's despond, in braille.

The girl at open half-door in her early Netherlandish light of melancholia.

So many brooding swans like floating inkstains on a lake of slender wakefulness.

Death as a German Expert

The North Star hanging
Like an umlaut over all of us, causes (even brittle) me to bend.

The weight of everything, bleak as babies in baskets
Rushing down the River Sauer toward their celestial misery.

I remember everything; my sister and I calling our mother person-
To-person in the afterlife. Always the dead will be lined as sad

And crookedly as fingerling potatoes in root-cellars dank enough
For overwintering. In Luckenwalde a young girl slides a needle

In the turnip-purple soft fold of her inner arm and this, too,
Transfigures to a kind of joy. Expertise is everything.

Angel, extinguish the tallows of the elder trees. (And he does.)
Death comes

Like another spotted foal born on the barn's cold floor,
Spindling to stand, and he does.

(TWO)

Gamine

Heart, be clean. Fists, be open, numb.
                              Most lovely

Lovely, let me be wrong in almost every
Thing. That the page is waste, all that rag

Content. That even despairing relentlessly cannot

Spare you what you fear the most.
                              Gamine, you are growing

Old now; it's your time. If you wait here
For the noises of this night,

They will sound out as the rustling of autumn,
                              Spiky, dried of unctuous

Airs, blazing like a chestnut horse on fire in
The padlocked barn;
                              It is time it will be time.

Morgue Near Heaven

If I imagine him healthy in his distressed
    Leather coat on someone's Sears plaid
Couch some years ago, then I will know
    All the nouns for shame he knows.

Perhaps I will write *green* as many times
    As he; he is affectionate about the spring;
I dread it as I dread the sulky pull of the season's
    Needle in its vein, drawing in.

I love him as I love all of the Dakotas,
    The two of them to which
I've never been, just as I've never really seen
    A death mask of his face,

Because, technically, he's never been
    That way, not yet.
If I keep his small triangle of a letter in his own
    Hand close to mine, then

Maybe I'll inherit all the Teutonic sentences
    He knows by heart, or all the same,
The grammar of the night, the factory
    Of slandering and fame.

The Insignificants

Tell me the story now in such
                         A way that I can hear it and still

Catch my breath. Rage is an aneurysm of the old animal
Brain, the reptilian gorge where nothing counts

But the body's urge & its boudoir
                         Of sulk and felt and shame.

Tell me I have heard tell there is a city
Where the graves float on the inconstant rain

Not fanciful, but accidental, actual—like milkstone
Spirits perched atop the smallest unbound human

Forms who died as insignificants.
                         For me, it is too late in the story

To die young, or guileless. I'd wanted once to love
Your mouth on mine, its ether

                         Gasping through a gauzy
Metal mask; I'd wanted to be breathed and taken

To an actual, like an addict floating on a desperate tiny river

Of open iridescent pigeons' wings and the floating poplin

                         Smocks of dusky, spoony girls.
As if I could breathe still.

A Lion in Winter

As long as the lions are rampant, I will stay
With him.
         As long as the clouded leopards

Surround the clouded bed with their gold & cirrus
Air, I will be there too. I was reading

When the winter shooed-
Away the fall and whitely lit the oil lamps of early

Dark. The night was turret-shaped in childhood,
         A bunch of mint and mane and swale.

What will I be when he is husk
To himself,
         Some flax or ghost of lynx in later winter light.

Caravansary

Here, on the first accidental
Day of winter in the middle
Of the great design & hemp

Of fall, my careless heart
Would be an ice-freaked hall,
Ill-lit, a hostelry, silked & hallowed

All along the sovereign
Persian corridors. I am
Implacable, profoundly influenced

By nothing short of filament
Or pilgrimage & light-piqued
Hours—portalled, saint-freaked, coy.

It will not be given to me, in this
Scurvy life, to speak
This time, of caravans of salt, or joy.

Common Swan on Ornamental Pond

And where are you now, my posthumous.
         Have you been bad, unplugging
The blue appliance cord that keeps you juiced into this
         World, particular with myrrh and bile?
         Have you risen wild
From your bed of straw floating on the curious island
         Of your room, descending sleek
As a demi-god assuming the form
         Of a pigeon hawk, late, in a swannery?
I am so moved by you I cannot help but speak.

Boy at the Border of His Own Allegory

A boy phones from a Frankish-
Speaking manor in Flanders, in the rain,

    To tell me he has a shotgun
    Muzzle to the inside

Of his Romance-speaking
Mouth. I tell him, take it from that ragged

    North Sea lair and put it to
    The milk and honey coffer

Of your chest and hold it silo-
Still and reddening there.

    It isn't speaking that you wanted to be quit

    Of, but only just to stop the sadiron

    Heavy flooding of the figure

    Of your inconstant, northing heart.

Like a madrigal, a pastoral
In the pocket of my houndstooth vest,

You are the only beauty in this
Celestial torture I will call my own.

Still Life with Feral Horse

It is love and its relinquish
I am discussing here,
A sorrel horse loosed

On a salt marsh island
Pelted by high storms,
And furious. He will not

Be handled by human
Hands, not in this given life
Of gratitude and tallow lamps

And famous churlishness.
I have heard tell
That you know how
To kill a man.

Self-Portrait on the Grassy Knoll

The only real place to gather consolation
Is from the back-talk of the dead, and they
          Do not speak to me.
Miss Jean Hill, the lady in red who named the hummock
"Grassy Knoll" in Abraham Zapruder's grainy film is
          Dead tonight at sixty-nine.

          In her red rain coat, she had been hoping
To loom small and pleasing on the glassy hill
          Like a poppy anemone in bloom.
Everything, of course, is colored now by what it was
I wanted then, but I am telling you I can't recall
          A time when I was that pretty or unharmed.

          The schoolguard in her yellow slicker
Crossing us toward home
Too early in that afternoon, in rain
          Some honeybees
In a field of mustardseed
          Flickering like radium or memory.

          Wait, anemic slippery light, let
Me hold onto your shadows as I would hold onto the hem
Of the sorcerer's tattered cloak after he has given up
          The ghost, departing
This one room for the world
          Of fact and time and black and white.

Soul Keeping Company

The hours between washing and the well
Of burial are the soul's most troubled time.

I sat with her in keeping company
All through the affliction of the night, keeping

Soul constant, a second self. Earth is heavy
And I made no wish, save being

Merely magical. I am magical
No more. This, I well remember well.

In the sweet thereafter the impress
Of the senses will be tattooed to

The whole world ravelling in the clemency
Of an autumn of Octobers, all that bounty

Bountiful and the oaks specifically
Afire as everything dies off, inclining

To the merciful. I would have made of my body
A body to protect her, anything to keep

Her well & here—in the soul's suite
Before five tons of earth will bear

On her, stay here
Soul, in the good night of my company.

(THREE)

Self-Portrait with Her Hair on Fire

Now, it is as dark as the pathos of pushing a wheel-
Chair through the museum of a great metropolis.

I cannot tell you this, not now, not ever, even
In the letter I have written that is so epic

That if you were to open it, the pages would sail out
In the wind like confection moths being born

In the thousands out of their sacks, blowing
Away, page by page, in a wind the color of her hair

Across a medieval pillow endlessly scorched,
The singe of something living tinged with fire.

I will go on loving as I love the backs
                Of things and the invisible,

As I love the hideous or an attention
                So attentive it is next to worshipping.

Brochure on Eden

I want to call things as they are: *madness*—
Callous, eventual mutants assuming our place in the sun,

Shiny, longing, dying young.
Here, waistcoat would stand for—*waistcoat,*

Your hunter paisley one, your green adulterated sackcloth
Of a once great-cloak.

                          Things as they really are:

It is Thursday and I want to die
Later. Doctor—the phlox in the fields are afire, hectic

As a brilliant patient strapped wildly in a cotton Union suit,
My fever-few, my Houdini, my—eventual,

                          This is finally, *the world.*

This world is a world as curious as the man
In his worsted top-coat found face down

In a cold lake last November, chaffy, husky,
Glume-nettles cased him like a snuffbox, surrounded

By ironwood leaves, in a brittle
Of boughs a little north of here,

In a New England which will always be
A gorgeous gloomy place to see

                          This gaudy time of year.

Fata Morgana

And here, in the red room
Of my Beaux Arts and my irony, all the fetishes will be safe

And in their places like the hummingbird who lives here

With me, just out of
Reach. Pray then to leave here in my own sweet bed with

All my charges safe from harm.
I was steadfast, had a taxidermist's patience to replicate

Each animal in proper form in after-life.
Exactitude was my genius, though I was inexact, or wrong,

In fact, and like my Captain kept
My men a little hungry on a diet of mirage and pumpkin,

Cabbages and salted pork,
And all they ever wanted, in the end, was kindness, praising,

And the limes. In a time
Of scurvy and especially at high sea, let me die here

On a widow-slickened night, having done
All the proper and romantic things,

The lemon custard and the lying still

In lemon light, the dried red Liar-

Roses strewn all around my Renaissance Revival bed,
When for the last time,

I will not wake not
Even from the mutiny of abiding humming dreams

That wakened me for
Years of mornings by the yellow light which harms me so.

The Deerhunting

We were preparing to miss our President and his
                    Long resplendent, minky hands when

He is gone, when we will rue prosperity & youth blown
                    Off like a bard traipsing past

                    Dusk under a hunter's moon.
Regarding suffering: if it is all technique

                    And not a drop of substance,
Don't bother coming home. The last owl of

October was perched here, on the tiny antler
                    Of my dream, obsolete as a flintlock

Gun, and camouflaged by the wisdom
                    Of a jumpy age. In the chat room

Of your fluorescent orange imagination, you will
                    Find me lying in

                    The saddle between two saw-
Tooth mountains like a swamp deer

Out of bedding, in the rain. Regarding rain:
                    I hunt for it, its rut & arch, its tracks

That splash the slippery creek past weepy
                    Willows near the slough.

And by winter, our new President will be muzzle-
                    Loading the wrong dark men

                    In a long dark jerrybuild of robes.
Even the fawn bag limits have been reached,

                    And the lung shots shot & the harvesting
Of fallow deer will be done by Tuesday night.

By November, the tines of my deepest thoughts will be "in
        Velvet." And I, the mother of nothing, mother

Of nothing at all, will spook, be
        Loving still, but just the same, the same.

Elsewhere

I had wanted for a moment to keep still
Like the Lindbergh baby who left this world, likewise,

Lulled into a childish stirless form, as he was gone on
                    His small way to elsewhere then.

Somewhere else, tonight,
                    The first to go is sleep.

The second, some realities.
                    Thirdly, I had loved,

I thought, with all my heart, but intermittently
Like inclement weather: unseasonably cool.

Regarding warmth: elsewhere
                    The night is Promethean

With punishment, elaborate as the Tower of the Winds
Constructed in the second century.

It is now the Lighthouse for the Clouds, still in and of
The air. Elsewhere each hour

                    Was a mercy and is spent.
The raids on others' wants went on.

Roads in autumn will continue to be carnal roads,
Else I would be keeping still, living on & on

Redundant in your sleep, endlessly unreasonably warm,
                    Elsewhere in and of the air.

Darwinism as Spite

The heart is a place made slippery
    As a minnow confused out

Of its school and caught on
A plaid pink dishtowel forty years ago

In Canada, startled as a hood-shy
      Falcon seized in

Flight, bewildered as a mine pony
      Sudden, taken up

From an underground of shale
Into the hinter of stark light,

Blinded by an eye accustomed only to
An underworld of bower, lake, or coal.

    Why was none of this written down?

Another Night in Khartoum

A sack of bees

Like a cataract
Opens, tangling its skein, filling the room

With the heavy machinery
Of honey and anatomies, and light.

Now the old silt
And the waterwheel of work, in cools of cave,

On further shore.

When the potter wasps gather
In their nests of clay, they will make a noise

Inconstant as the White Nile
Where it meets the Blue one

In the ruined evening of Khartoum,

Where a king's mouth fills with
                              Cowered weeds.

It was not enough to have
The very thing you love

Just for an attendant while, not even in that place

Where you could not stand
To be civilized.

Lady with an Ermine

In the snow, white noise, a gathering
Of foxes oddly standing still in the milk broth of oblivion.

In the keep at Castlestrange, an ermine pelt in the shape
Of an ermine animal, but empty, slung over the carved

Oak chair, carelessly & keeping no
One warm.

A Truce to Tragedy

                                Long the wind will be
            Tobacco-colored in its field of mere

            And war, and strong the mind as an unlovely
            Hunter, gathering

            The furrows of a singlesighted
            Life. Long the heart itself was fictive,

            Pleated like the corrugated roof
            Of the open mouth of a fantastical tragedy,

            Unfolded, too, like letters penned lying face-up in
            A bed of down and opium,

            A still-warm kit of reddish eggs beneath a newly
            Fallen snuff of snow, a rumination on

            What might not have been,
                                And long, but tenderly.

Fragment on Dissembling

Curious in your dark
Frock-coat, do everything
That you have to,
     If it is time;
     Leave nothing
Still unsaid.
Once, to make of nothing
Something, was divine.
     To have made
     Of something
Nothing, was sublime.

(FOUR)

The Halo That Lit Twice

Tell me where in what penultimate white
World do you imagine you can be quit

Of these
Blood-tied arteries which lead

Directly to the improbable thoracic
Cavity of me, what Department of Erotic

Wars, what Alexandria, what character-is-fate, what coven
Of intensive care, what raven-

Width, what upper GI bleed, what chamber
Of anatomy, what ice and vigory,

What breastplate, lymph, what coat
Of arms, what curious unspeakable, what one lamp left

On in the vaulted amber window of the Public Library
Where a cowled friar has been deep in study

Lucubrating like the patron saint of random births
And worthlessness,

An accidental light left all night
Long, pulsing slightly

Like the bundled one-ounce heart
Of an infant harvested, delivered here on ice,

Which began to flutter faintly
Like the halo that lit twice,

That lit and faltered, halted, lit
Once more, and then went out.

Self-Portrait as Kaspar Hauser

What was it like then?
> In my prison I thought of nothing.

What did you think of?
> Not boot or trouser, not the bearable
> Light or trough, not rain,
> Not bread or wagon, water, rain.

What was it like?
> The heart had I known I had one had folded
> In. As if an ox lay down in rue & hay.
> I lay still.

What did you think then?
> I was a scar. A scoop of swale.
> An applecart left out in an orchard.
> It is December now. Nothing.

Could you speak then?
> The white of the paper blinded me.

Could you speak aloud?
> I was a wonderment.

Were you able to speak?

> Once, I felt a joy. This was as old as beasts
> Of burden working, in the grainy field.
> A plough of good white speech.

> There was a toy in the shape of a small
> White horse. It was to me a living form.
> I was its equal, grief, the same grieved

Thing, wheeling & unworldly, wild as
Wheat. I will to be wandering in
The waving fields of eel-grass, as if

Underwater in the salt marsh of the moors.
A hatchet, flowering; a balky calf. As I touched
The flame I did not know how to flinch, but cried.

Apologue on Jealousy

The paddocks are now empty of wind and all
Nobility,
      And I am half sick of shadows, too.
You are lucky not to be afraid of dying, not of dying
Itself but of its
      Way, how much it may hurt
Like the lugubrious
Hundred cellos bowing, burning
      In the caesarean ward some nights.

In the split-risk ward, the weird fate
      Of what remains
To be sent home is merely anatomical, but stained
Anonymous, as in an earlier world
War.
      Please deliver us this
Leaflet in a land hospitable to coveting, and pain.

Self-Portrait in the Miraculous
World, with Nimbed Ox

I had come home from my medieval
Universe where love lies

                Over the law,
Where possession is

Ten-tenths of all that life, lying
Like ten men in the draught, drawing air and skirting

The ploughlands like a domestic whore at home.
The heart is not

                A usual device.

He said: you cannot say,
                Cancers be gone,

                Heart be strong
                As a lion.

The New Realism
Will be a bovine one with widened eyes;

                Look about
You, in the foreground, some acts of posthumous

Miracles on their verge; all-bearing
Nature was my fictive frame.

Heart be strong as a burden beast,
                Common, clumsy, sunlit, oxish, kind.

Almost a Conjuror

The slight white poet would assume non-human forms, homely
Grampus fish, a wahoo, nuthatch, nit.

                                    He had no romance except
Remorse, which he used like fuzzy algebra. By pouring bluing

On black porous coal, he crystallized, pronounced himself almost
A sorcerer. He had an empty cloakroom

                                    In the chest of him.
                                    All the lost wool scarves

Of all the world collected there & muffled him
                                    With wool.

He imagined he could move a broom if he desired, just by wishing
It. If he spoke of ghosts, he thought he could make of art vast

                                    Tattersall & spreading wings.
When they found him in the nurse's office,

He was awkward as a charlatan, slightly queasy
                                    In an emperor's real clothes.

The thermos in his lunchbox was perpetually
Broken and he lied. The small world smelled of oil

Of peppermint, for a broken spell. Everything is plaid
                                    And sour in oblivion, as well.

Self-Portrait with Self-Pity

In the principalities
Of desire, retention of power

Is everything, even at the cost of treachery.
I know this much as one

Familiar with the jack-keeping off
Of the barbarians outside the city's iron gate.

I'm telling you, my bleak, all
Winter long, it will be mercilessly

Iced here now, the frost is cold-cock
Cloven vixen prints on metal railroad tracks,

The trains go on and on
With their whistling, with their tupelo cargo,

Their serious & pitiless,
Their limber want, their gloom.

Girl at the Border of Her Own Allegory

A man takes off his armor past the Iron Age
And it stands without

       The man inside;
She folds in

The metal garments of his great blank
Wings of winter. In

Saint Petersburg, the night-
Engraving churchbells toll and in this

Constant cold I do not know
If tolling signifies

A death or marrying, hollowed
Out of frost, or rue, or injury.

       The dark is big, filling
       The city with silver

       And trouble. You are colder
Where you are,

Love, curious as the alchemist who keeps
His salamander living in a flask of fire, while

The will of me, a black reptilian
Doctor's bag, clicks shut.

                  My own fealty galls,
Bewilders me.

In Cocteau, to La Bête's white horse, the Beauty says:
Go where I am going. And he takes me there.

Of the Finished World

Open the final book: November spills
Its lamplit light, the clenched astronomer

Hunched at table, considering his vexed
Celestial map, illegible as the flinch

Of needles falling on the blanched
Rye fields in pentagrams.

The harvest is done with itself, its ransack
Done. The wild-coated horses bunch

In the clot of darkness that falls on the land.
In the twice-ploughed field, picked

Clean, what is left of the bottle-gourds
Will freeze by night, a throttled hour

From here. On the freighted road, laden with
Old hunger and apocrypha, a heaven sloughs

Its midden things, things left of the unfinished
World, its most hideous & permanent

Impermanence. I was not awake
For any war to speak of.

          In the finished world
I will be wind-awry, will be out

          Of mind, in asylum
Where even the astronomer will no longer

Attend to the world undone.
How have I lived here so long?

In Elsinore

There would be a boy

Insensible in fog
On an afternoon when lamps are hung

Even in mid-day

For the sake of those still travelling.
There would be a stray

Of music fashioned from a horsehair

Bow drawn across the torso
Of the cello's form.

In Elsinore where everything

Is probable, he would not die there
Like a child

But like a child he had wished to die.

The tide moves deeper
In and handsomely as Denmark sleeps

Collectively in wool.

For the sake of those still travelling
Who live so far & crookedly from

Here, I would not stay strangely

Like a child,
But like a child I have been astray.

Spain

The god-leash leaves
Its lashes on the broad bunched backs

Of sacrificial animals. The whippings stain

Even the muslin of the streets with bright red poppies

On this Sunday morning when the wedding

Would have been as full-blown as the cotton crop
In the hour

Before it's plucked from its scratchy little hulls.

I can say "little"

Now as many times as I goddamn
Want, here in the hour of my forty years & four,

Here beneath the hardback hour of my death or
Past as it will *really* happen here,

And then the saltwater's salt and its "heal" and sting,
This unholy lovely strapping

Thing, annulled. You will find me then,

A little damp, in

My small Madrid of shame.

(FIVE)

Portrait of Lucy with Fine Nile Jar

My torso is a cedar chest in the brief closet
Of the middle of a country, hollow

                Until three young sisters
Curl there like marsupials and shut

The bevelled door and die there,
                Not determined yet, into

The camphored pouch of an Otherworld.
Around this death there was a fine Nile jar

Of halo-light, where I am
                Thinking of you now,

                Everything; you're all
                Over;

Out of time like a nightjar
In the diorama of the great hall

Of prehistory, depicting the tiny cataclysmic
                Moment of some mythic, leggy

Accident that changed the world
One day, numinous as a Petrarchan

Sunflower in the night. A moment
                Perfect as a bee suspended

In the perfect weather of a honey jar.
Your heart was cinctured, full, surrounded

By a hinder of restharrow
                Roots, nestled in its little parasol

Portrait of Lucy with Fine Nile Jar

Of amber grief, willful as a wooden tiger standing
        In an empty yellow room.

While you were leaving, I was lying, eastward,
On my back, like a pharaoh counting

The layers of muslin wound
Around my cumbrous (nearly human)

Hand, counting the days until
        An evermore arrives.

The Identity of the Bridegroom

One night you will walk into a flume
Of the great Mississippi River with your blue

Malthusian urge, in a gluey
                Great-coat of a great

Inertia, and go down into the runnelled
Underworld, standing still as a pale suitor

Handing blossoms to a girl with queen

Yellow jackets in her hair I swear
You will. I am tired

Of women who are sad. I am tired
                Of men who are tired.

You are unwholesome mantling
The river in this
                Ochre-wedded light.

Self-Portrait as a Herd of One

The reason why I love the orchard is my propensity for lavish
Order in certain seasons of the year, when a Glaswegian

Gloom ascends as snow apples fall long before the snow is
Come. When she died, it might as well have spooned the quince-

Shaped heart from me. Forgiveness, in this agnostic time, was
Not a possibility, the way each pome-fruit orchard was

A whole tin bucket of despairs, singly as benign as
Silvernerve, in accumulation something powerful and poisonous.

A hearse moves through the city like a herd of
One, bison-like and woolly in the summer sun, carnivorous.

Recall the kitchen and your half-learned love, the room you know
She will never be inside again, and someone telling you:

She is not here, she is not anywhere, you see, and you were there;
It was the last time you would be at home, in harm.

Physicism

In the valley of the Euphrates, each
Of the stars had certain shepherds

To the people there. Here, in this small valley
Showered with emboli, we each have none.

Before the Babylonians, the sun was called
Old Sheep, the planets Old Sheep Stars.

There are blood-sheep everywhere,
But no shepherds left.

      Only blood sisters here,
All with the color taken from their sight.

We live in black & white, material
And motherless beneath the concavity of sky.

Phenomenal on the long aortic pulse
Of equinox, a Sumerian describes his stars

Collectively as *flock* and it is heavenly to him.
Here there is no heaven here.

Pyrrhic Victory

When you have won, good voyager, your pilgrimage will be
Calamitous as a victory

Got by slashing and burning your own tailored fields of gold.

A cocoon will bloom in the empty chest of the beloved, lavishly.

I do not want to be a chrysalis again.
How long will I have to live here quickened in

My finespun case, like a folded pilgrim, blushing,
Till I am moth.
.
The nightmares have come back
Like women winding their hair in sullen braids, untroubling

As the sound of flour being sifted onto parchment, shifting
As it winnows itself.

Powder is dread, refined.
The imperative: to win.

And all this happened after keeping mute for many years

Like a sallow box of baking soda with no expiration date,

Innocuous, absorbing everything.
Some grief is larger than my body is.

Self-Portrait with Her Hair Cut Off

Like the Shropshire clock with its pocked off-white face
        Of Roman numerals as it wound down, the night will

Be as still as the garden of wildflowers and pinking
        Shears I wandered into once that many years before all

My hair was scissored off for punishment, a love so struck
        It might have slain you with its magnitude: the sack

Of dust called "Long Ago."
        In the pillow of swill I call "Now,"

The past happens over and over again like a kingfisher
        Veering off its destined course, and hovering.

                    Promise yourself just this
One thing: do not strive to be exceptional.

There will be hours for that in the hackneyed
        Looming after, and the afterwards.

The One Thousand Days

There is the mourning dish of salt
Outside my door, a cup of quarantine, saucerless, a sign

That one inside has been taken down
By grieving, ill tongue-tied will, or simple illness,

                              Yet trouble came.
I have found electricity in mere ambition,

If nothing else, yet to make myself sick on it,
A spectacle of marvelling & discontent.

Let me tell you how it came to this.
I was turning over the tincture of things,

I was trying to recollect the great maroon
Portière of everything that had ever happened,

When the light first stopped its transport
And the weather ceased to be interesting,

Then the dark drape closed over the altar
And a minor city's temple burnt to ground.

I was looking to become inscrutable.
I was longing to be seen through.

It was at slaughtering, it was at the early
Stain of autumn when the dirt-tinted lambs

Were brought down from the high
Unkempt fields of Sligo, bidden, unbidden, they

Came down. It was then that I was
Quit of speech, a thousand northbound nights of it.

Then was ambition come
Gleaming up like a fractured bone as it breaks

Through the bodiced veil of skin.
I marry into it, a thistle on the palm, salt-pelt on

The slaughtering, and trouble came.
That the name of bliss is only in the diminishing

(As far as possible) of pain. That I had quit
The quiet velvet cult of it,
                                        Yet trouble came.

Dire Wolf

Sorrows, like a gathering of dire wolves, come in packs. To you,
I am not speaking anymore. Whom

Shall I address?

Now that you have gotten these things off
Your barrel chest, it is time for you to merge into the sobbing

Rain, like a one-room scene in Appalachia, smeared
By fog. I adored you as much as an aluminum

Bucket of storm after
A great unlovely silvered thirst. How

Nice for me. In the Pleistocene, the wild wolves roamed
In scattered sorrows over

Everywhere, prodigious in appetite, howling
At the hollow of

Everything empty like a throat coated
With the fabric of a bolt

Of red. There

Are things which can dismantle entirely
A spirit, such as the pathetic maledictive fear

Of loss. Of loss:
You get to speak of it, once

You are its intimate, and not before; it would be
"Appropriation." But in the great white rendezvous, where

I was brooding
Just a while, you get to speak of dire love.

Pamphlet on Ravening

You cannot will intoxication, vertigo, a ravening or wild
                    Love. Of wisdom, I have plenty,

Like a keep of potted meats before the blizzard comes.
                    Of sweetness, I've a bowl of plenty too,

Though it's against the law to harbor wonder

In the prison of the Post-Hellenic world where
                    I move easily
Miraculous and moving

                    On the slower barge
Up the River Hubris in the post-curiouser world.
                    Wondrous:

I was a hunger artist once, as well.
                    My bones had shone.
                    I had had rapture on my side.

Self-Deliverance by Lion

To maul is to make a massive loss
Of the history of a body's history.

What will be taken will be the custody
Of soft tissue, and astonishment.

Her hair was a long damp chestnut
River-pelt spilled after an enormous

And important rain. Her body was still sticky
With the lilac repetitions in her cotton dress.

She was found face-up on a cold March morning
By the most menial and tender of the keepers

At the zoo, crewelled with frost marks, cursive
As the dewclaws on a lion's forepaw, massive

And significant. I had hoped for, all that Serengeti
Year, a hopelessness of less despair

Than hope itself. I knew the excellent repair
Of night fell cruel and quickly where

The lions had the mastery of me—aware
Their mastery was by my will, and fair.

Notes

In a small notebook called "Pieces of Paper," Wallace Stevens transcribed several hundred titles for poems which he never wrote. From this journal, I've adapted the following: "The Halo That Would Not Light," "Still Life with Aspirin," "The One Theme of Which Everything Else Is a Variation," "Basic Poem in a Basic Tongue," "Morgue Near Heaven," "Brochure on Eden," "Darwinism as Spite" (from "Communism as Spite"), "A Truce to Tragedy," and "The Identity of the Bridegroom."

Stevens's notebook is reproduced in George S. Lensing's *Wallace Stevens: A Poet's Growth* (Baton Rouge and London: Louisiana State University Press, 1986).

In **Still Life with Aspirin,** the line *For a poem to be true, it must "come from an Ever"* has as its source the following transcription from Stevens's notebook:

> *Qualities of a poem*
> > interesting
> > indigenous to a person
> > d'un daemon
> > felt words
> > capable of infuriating
> > with
> > poetry emotion
> > to come from an ever
> > free source
> > esser [*sic*]: [*essor* (Fr.); swarm or group flight]
> > effortless
> > contagious

Some of the language in **Leaflet on Wooing** is drawn from the Seventh of Rilke's *Duino Elegies*. In the Stephen Mitchell translation, the poem begins: *Not wooing, no longer shall wooing, voice that has outgrown it, / be the nature of your cry.*

The title **Death as a German Expert** is adapted from a line in John Berryman's "Dream Song No. 41."

The title **Almost a Conjuror** is from Yannis Ritsos, *Testimonies I,* translated by Kimon Friar.

The phrase **Soul Keeping Company** refers to an ancient Jewish mourning ritual. According to tradition, even after death, the soul stays hovering until the body itself is properly buried. The body cannot be left alone for even an hour, and guardians must keep constant vigil, affording company for the soul during its most difficult time.

Fata Morgana describes a kind of mirage produced by continually changing reflections of light on water, most frequently seen in the Strait of Messina. These lights were attributed in early times to the agency of the fairy Morgan, sister of King Arthur.

Herculaneum was the ancient city in Campania, which was destroyed, together with Pompeii, by the eruption of Vesuvius in A.D. 79.

Kaspar Hauser was the name given to the child who, on Whit-Monday 1828, mysteriously appeared in the town square of Nuremberg. He was feral and had no speech save one sentence: "I would like to be a horseman like my father." He would take only bread and water. Eventually, the boy became the ward of Ritter Anselm von Feuerbach until, in 1833, Kaspar was attacked and stabbed to death by an unknown assailant.

The close of **Girl at the Border of Her Own Allegory** is based on Jean Cocteau's 1946 film, *La Belle et la Bête.* At the Beast's High Gothic castle, he keeps a white stallion with a tinseled mane. The horse, Magnificat, can transport its rider to any imagined destination without instruction or direction.

The opening image in **The One Thousand Days** refers to the Japanese custom of placing a dish of salt outside the front door of the home where a family member has recently died.

The largest known species of wolf, the **Dire Wolf,** roamed the North American continent until its extinction during the Pleistocene period.

The title **Self-Deliverance by Lion** is adapted from Kay Redfield Jamison's *Night Falls Fast*. In 1995, the body of a thirty-six-year-old transient woman from Little Rock was discovered by a worker at the National Zoo in Washington. She had scaled a barrier, ascended a rough high wall, and crossed a twenty-six-foot moat in order to make her way into the lions' den. Her death by mauling was ruled a suicide.

From Daniel 6:24, I've adapted the following: *The lions had the mastery of them / And broke all their bones in pieces.*

The Halo That Would Not Light is for Lucy Grealy.
Periodic Table of Ethereal Elements is for Harry Ford.
Soul Keeping Company is for my mother, Ginger Greenwald.
Self-Portrait in the Miraculous World, with Nimbed Ox is for Richard Howard.
Self-Portrait as a Herd of One is for Timothy Donnelly.
The One Thousand Days is for James Miller.
Physicism is for my sisters, Julie Broido Parmenter and Melissa Greenwald.

And gratitude, abiding, to Frank Bidart, Sophie Cabot Black,
Mark Doty, Deborah Garrison, Richard Locke, Liam Rector, Jason Shinder,
Tree Swenson, Benjamin Taylor, Helen Vendler, and Alan Ziegler.

Acknowledgments

The author wishes to thank the editors of the journals
in which versions of these poems have appeared.

THE AMERICAN POETRY REVIEW: *Another Night in Khartoum; Basic Poem in a Basic Tongue; Brochure on Eden; Caravansary; Girl at the Border of Her Own Allegory; The Halo That Lit Twice; Herculaneum; The Insignificants; Lady with an Ermine; A Lion in Winter; Morgue Near Heaven; Pamphlet on Ravening; Self-Portrait as a Herd of One; Some Details of Hell; Spain; Still Life with Aspirin; Still Life with Feral Horse; A Truce to Tragedy*

THE BOSTON REVIEW: *Boy at the Border of His Own Allegory; Gamine; Portrait of Lucy with Fine Nile Jar*

THE MAKING OF A POEM: A NORTON ANTHOLOGY OF POETIC FORMS (ed. by Mark Strand and Eavan Boland, New York: W.W. Norton & Co., 2000): *Of the Finished World*

COLORADO REVIEW: *Physicism; Self-Portrait in the Miraculous World, with Nimbed Ox; Self-Portrait with Self-Pity*

DAEDALUS: *The One Thousand Days*

DENVER QUARTERLY: *Common Swan on Ornamental Pond; Darwinism as Spite; Fragment on Dissembling*

HARVARD PHI BETA KAPPA POEM 2001: *Self-Portrait as Kaspar Hauser*

MARGIE: THE AMERICAN JOURNAL OF POETRY: *In Elsinore*

THE NATION: *Soul Keeping Company*

THE NEW REPUBLIC: *The Identity of the Bridegroom*

THE NEW YORKER: *The Halo That Would Not Light*

THE PARIS REVIEW: *Death as a German Expert; Fata Morgana; Periodic Table of Ethereal Elements*

PARNASSUS: POETRY IN REVIEW: *After Raphael; The One Theme of Which Everything Else Is a Variation; Pyrrhic Victory; Self-Deliverance by Lion*

SALMAGUNDI: *Apologue on Jealousy; Self-Portrait with Her Hair Cut Off; Self-Portrait with Her Hair on Fire*

SLATE: *Almost a Conjuror; Dire Wolf; Leaflet on Wooing*

THE THREEPENNY REVIEW: *Self-Portrait on the Grassy Knoll*

VOLT: *The Deerhunting; Elsewhere*

A Note About the Author

Lucie Brock-Broido is the author of two previous collections of poetry, *A Hunger* and *The Master Letters*. She is Director of Poetry in the School of the Arts at Columbia University. She has been the recipient of awards from the John Simon Guggenheim Foundation, the National Endowment for the Arts, and the American Academy of Arts and Letters. She lives in New York City and in Cambridge, Massachusetts.

A Note on the Type

This book was set in Granjon, a type named in compliment to Robert Granjon, a type cutter and printer active in Antwerp, Lyons, Rome, and Paris from 1523 to 1590. Granjon, the boldest and most original designer of his time, was one of the first to practice the trade of typefounder apart from that of printer.

Linotype Granjon was designed by George W. Jones, who based his drawings on a face used by Claude Garamond (ca. 1480–1561) in his beautiful French books. Granjon more closely resembles Garamond's own type than do any of the various modern faces that bear his name.

Composed by Creative Graphics,
Allentown, Pennsylvania

Printed and bound by United Book Press,
Baltimore, Maryland

Printed in the United States
by Baker & Taylor Publisher Services